WestBow Press books may be ordered through booksellers or by contacting:

WestBow Press
A Division of Thomas Nelson & Zondervan
1663 Liberty Drive
Bloomington, IN 47403
www.westbowpress.com
844-714-3454

Interior Image Credit: Carol Bicknell

ISBN: 979-8-3850-3838-1 (sc)
979-8-3850-3839-8 (hc)
979-8-3850-3837-4 (e)

Library of Congress Control Number: 2024924869

Print information available on the last page.

WestBow Press rev. date: 12/18/2024

WESTBOW
PRESS®
A DIVISION OF THOMAS NELSON
& ZONDERVAN

The Wondrous Seasons of Our Lives

By Ronald William Cadmus

Illustrations By Carol Bicknell

Ralph Waldo Emerson wrote:

"Never lose an opportunity of seeing anything that is beautiful; for beauty is God's handwriting—a wayside sacrament. Welcome it in every fair face, in every fair sky, in every fair flower, and thank God for it as a cup of blessing."

Albert Camus wrote:

"In the middle of winter, I at last discovered that there was in me an invincible summer."

Table of Contents

A *Dedication*

For The Wondrous Seasons of Our Lives

After all the years of my living, a memory, a face, a special friendship, the never ending flow of the treasured moments that gave my life meaning, swirl within the heart springs of my affections for all that has touched my life. As time goes on, as seasons change, the constant aspect of love flows through it all. We are gifted with life, by those who created us, by those who shared their love with us and shaped us through all the aspects of their being and sharing. To all these moments, all these memories and the hearts of those who reside in my life – a depth of gratitude I give to each one.

I think of my grandfather, Basil Bacatselos, an immigrant as a young boy from Greece, who was nurtured in his growing years in the beautiful hills of the Peloponnese mountain ranges in Southern Greece. His life affected me as a young boy growing up in the city of Newark, NJ. My grandfather kept me connected to the ground, literally, in all its changing seasons. He taught me to be still in woodlands, quiet under cathedral trees reaching towards the skies. I can hear him say to me today, as we walked in the woods, "Be still and listen to the running streams." He put his fingers to his lips and then to his ear and said, "Shhhh, listen to the new snowflakes, with their kissing sounds on the crisp, autumn leaves in winter's first snowfall on the forest floor." He would tenderly hold a budding flower in his fingertips and never pick it. He would hold twigs of Rosemary in his hands and smell their fragrance, reminding him of the herbs in the fields of his village home in Greece. Through all the wondrous, changing seasons of life, I remember those precious moments that simply came from simply living. I'm still following streams, following dreams, feeling the sun's warm rays filtering through cathedral trees. I remember and am grateful for many things. Richly blessed from being touched by him and so many through all the changing years. And to think, that God holds it all together in God's hands. I pray that a word in this book will bring you to those places that are wondrous in their memories of all the seasons of your lives. And to my dear Grandfather who is long gone from this earth, I hold you in my heart, very tightly, closely, and sense the fragrance of your love, and hear your words of wisdom to reach my hands within those cool mountain streams and splash myself with life!

$\mathscr{F}$orward

"In **_The Wondrous Seasons of Our Lives_** the reader finds purpose, faith, and themselves in the ever-changing seasons. Unhurried pacing and bits of nostalgia woven with reality made this a warm read that I will revisit again and again. Ronald Cadmus' exquisite word painting coupled with his neighbor Carol Bicknell's abstract impressionistic illustrations create a perfect artistic pairing. This beautiful book of poetry will slow your world down just a bit as you rediscover creation and its Creator.

Heather Sorenson

Heather Sorenson entered the church music industry in her twenties, and her name quickly became a welcomed fixture in the publishing world. Heather is hired by the largest and most respected publishers in the world, and her pieces remain at the top of Bestsellers lists and Editor's Choice selections.

Diversity is the characteristic that makes Heather somewhat of an anomaly in the industry: she easily maneuvers both the traditional and contemporary genres of Christian music, often combining the two for a unique blend that has become her artistic fingerprint. Initially recognized for her skill as a pianist, Heather is now known for her compositions in choral anthems, solo piano collections, and orchestrations. Her works are performed regularly at competitions, concerts, recitals, and churches worldwide. Over the past several years, Heather has appeared multiple times at Carnegie Hall, Lincoln Center, and Constitution Hall in the roles of pianist and composer.

Years of experience as a church music administrator and music educator have proven to be invaluable experience, and teaching has become a large part of Heather's ministry. She taught all elementary levels of music at Grace Academy of Dallas for 4 years, served as an adjunct music professor at Baylor University, and has served on many master class panels in piano and songwriting. Heather regularly is a guest speaker and conductor at churches across America, and leads scores of sessions each year at various worship conferences, schools and universities.

Endorsement

JEFFREY SIGER Is a Best Selling Mystery Writer. He is published in the US, UK, Germany (German), Bulgaria, and Greece (Greek and English), and has served as Chair of the National Board of Bouchercon, the world's largest mystery convention, and as Adjunct Professor of English at Washington & Jefferson College, teaching mystery writing.

Jeffrey Siger says about "The Wondrous Seasons of Our Lives" - ***"Move Over Vivaldi"***

Preface

The future is so near
As each approaching second
Brings "tomorrow" into "now"
Then steps into the "past."
Moments, each that birth a dream, come true, remembered:
Eternity, imagination, the chronicles of time,
all live and move
in thoughts we breathe, inhaling innovations in
the whispers of an instant, in the wondrous seasons of our lives.
Time speaks to us in silent thoughts
stirs the mind to gaze at stars
and blaze a trail
upon the constellations,
in just three moments.
We seek the dawn that breaks
with new discoveries
that lead us to conceive
what life can be.
Within our mind,
our soul,
our heart,
is bursting
the brilliant light
so we might see what yet can be.

Light lives and moves
in thoughts we breath, inhaling innovations in
the whispers of an instant.
Time speaks to us in silent thoughts
stirs the mind to gaze at stars
and blaze a trail
upon the constellations,
in just three moments.
Fresh dreams and passions,
surprising myst'ries
like wings unfolding in a chrysalis
or preserved in a crystal snowflake
things unimagined
reveal their secrets
and vow their sweet betrothal with a kiss.
Learn from the lessons
of the past
to make the world a better place.
Shape your visions
to inspire
all the human race,
and live,
and live,
and live
the promise of three moments
As we move through the wondrous seasons of our lives.
Through all of our lives, these moments merge together
So that we are never without the changing seasons of our lives
Enshrined within each moment of our lives.

It is through my words in this book that I hope you find God's presence in
Each instant – the beauty, the creativity, the promise, the hopes, every dream,
Every desire, every touch of the Creator's hand and heart
To fill your lives with wondrous moments. The seasons change,
We live and move and have our being
And marvel at the beauty of the seasons we are seeing.
They come and go, each with something of the wondrous promise that
In each moment we find life in all its fullness
And in the end to know
The constant, unchanging nature of God's love
To find the gift of love and life that makes each moment
Wondrous and worth living.

Ronald W. Cadmus

xiv

The Promise of the Solstice Sun

Turning slightly toward the sun
Each day is lengthened,
A cosmic solstice yearning,
So we can hold light longer.
The joy born, with each ray of dawn,
Longs to seep into our heart.
Birds fly from green lawns
and blossomed trees
and soar to higher skies
with sun beams nesting on their wings.
We want to fly, lofty like them
In search of dreams we can believe.
In the pirouette toward the summer sun
We hum a melody our hearts can sing!
New life to caress
When we feel unregimented!
Summer days, starlit nights, displays of happiness,
A Pas de Deux in the ballet of our play
On carefree, dancing days.
Having fun,
In the summer sun.

Longer days, and shorter nights
when earth twists slightly toward the sun
Give shadows, cast on the wall,
less time to tango with our fears in the dark.
The early sunrise
The late sunset
Extend the light
Revealing, the metronome beat of time, of how to effusively live,
If we choose to rotate toward the solstice sun.
The sandy beach awaits our footsteps
Waves reach to catch us so we can sail
Their crest to bright horizons.
Mountain trails, nature hikes,
bike excursions,
getting out of boring ruts, exploring the coves
along placid lakes,
drifting on tubes, casting fish line for summer diversions
relaxing by cool, graceful streams.
Daring to ride down whitewater canyons
Having the audacity, having the guts.
Children in their playful times,
Converting sheets and clotheslines into tents and huts.
Hitting baseballs, running bases, games of tag,

seeking wonders, where they hide.
Family outings, back yard picnics
swings in the park reaching high,
Strolls around our neighborhoods
And city streets
Greeting neighbors we rarely meet.
Summer gives bright light to find each other.
More time for love. More love for life!
In a stranger find a sister, brother.
Lazy days in hammocks,
The scent of nature after rain.
Moonlight walks and crickets chirping
Cicadas in nocturnal cadence,
Joining in late night porch conversations.
Taking that overdue vacation.
Fireflies surprise appearance among the trees, shooting stars in ebony skies.
Breathing places for our soul, the solstice sun,
Sharing treasures and bags of gold.
We can bask in blissful moments
If we let the light dilate our appreciation
As we turn our eyes
toward the promise of the
Solstice Sun shining in the summer sky.

The Mysterious Maturity of Autumn

Fields are rich for harvest
Hills and forests release their hidden colors
A tapestry of beauty before leaves fall
From the vibrant landscape.
In this passing season
We are reminded how things change,
Nothing remains the same.
The barren trees stretch their limbs and cry
As if to try to hold onto each
Leaf they fed.
Wrestling winds, they release, with sadness
The life they cannot keep.
It is a time of plenty, wheat waving in the fields
It is a time of dying
As seeds fall to the earth, awaiting their rebirth,
for something fresh to yield.
Each carried leaf upon the wind, waves to us its salutation,
And bequeath their thanks in a single tear drop of their sad goodbye.
The cycle leads to certain endings

In our mysterious creation.
What was lush and verdant
Separates itself from twigs upon a branch
That nourished it once with life.
Now crisp remains tossed by the shivering chill
Of autumn,
We know both its abundance,
As well as all its strife.
Yet the mystery of autumn
Is part of the design of fruitful bearing
That Autumn can provide.
To see the purpose in the maturing season,
To find meaning in the mellowing of our lives.
While it seems life is dying.
The cycle holds its reasons
To keep earth warm,
With an Indian Summer, like hope that never
Withdraws its promise,
That Autumn will keep us nourished, calm
Through the harsh days to come.
Chrysanthemums and asters in November
Help us remember
That this season holds a harvest.
Still something grows.
We mature in wisdom, we come to know
That through the changing scenes of life

The secrets of the season reveal an arcane truth
For our living.
Like the landscape changing color
We display new shades and pigments
Like barren trees, the hardening earth
Our bodies wrinkle, memory fades
Our hair turns gray and ashen,
Our bones become stiff, if not arthritic
We suffer loss, yet reap rich harvests
in the autumn season.
When loved ones on changing winds are carried away,
the mystery of autumn reveals a hopeful message:
The heart is the storehouse of our wisdom
Of all that we have learned.
Holding all that we have loved.
And in some distant, new beginning
We will see hints of green, new life, new promise
Upon the hills return.
As the kaleidoscope of the season,
In its turning
Reveals another image
So that we may stand in awe and wonder
Of the beauty of a deeper revelation that we find
Within our hearts,
Where wisdom has taught us to give thanks
in this season.

The Gifts of Winter

Crystal frost on window panes
The hush of country lanes
Sleighbells ringing on village streets
Fahrenheit turning rain to sleet
The blessed incense of fireplace logs,
aromatherapy from cottage roofs
wafting through the woods.
The pure white powder drifting 'round barren trees
soft mounds of nature's magic dust
Swirling, dancing in lamp post light
Revealing shadows of footprint lanes
Giving earth its peace at night.
A pathway we can trust.
These are the gifts of winter.
Nature sleeps in hibernation,
Waiting with anticipation
Plants and flowers repose, relax in preparation
For the miracle when a new season warms iron soil
Into softened transformation.
Frigid, cold, the air can sting
the blood beneath our cheeks,
With slaps against our face.
Winds howl and pluck the tree's brittle twigs

With subtle music like winter harps.
Allowing in arctic, midwinter days,
every heart to sing.
Sometimes the season has its blizzards
Is desolate and harsh
Sometimes more mild,
Clear crisp winter skies allow stars to
shine their brightest.
There is a sacred stillness in nature's duvet
That covers all the wintergreen
To give the earth a purity
That we can see each day
When all is chaos, bleak and gray.
Gently, all around us, flow the flurries of delight
That become garlands for the trees
As we play and catch the beauty of their design
Upon our tongues and eyelashes.
And with a childlike faith
Winter causes us to dream,
For the harshest winter wants us to know
That we can make the world a better place
If we ly down upon its gift and
make angel wings in the snow.

The Serenity of Snow

Nature can be gentle, kind
like soft snowflakes
to keep the flower warm beneath the frost
the seed hidden in the frozen dark
is obsessed with anticipation
that soon, in some other form,
it will awaken to the sun.
A broken heart can know
it will love again..
a brittle branch will bud
as birds return,
their silent voice bursting into song.
Till that moment,
a white quilt blankets the mind
with indulgent lullabies….
The serenity of snow….
the solemnity of soul….

crystals and secret songs of snowflakes
find a world of promise
beneath their gentle kiss,
that turns bleak moments
into unblemished purity.
In life's glacial moments,
its deepest hurts
and unknown reasons
we find the passion
of changing seasons
to keep on living,
as snow warms despair with hope
and lets the heart beat silently
where dreams are born
and leave their heart-prints in
the serenity of snow.

The Eternal Spring In Us

The rhapsody of creation
Awakens from its winter sleep,
Calling slumbering spirits from repose
To deeper mysteries of our communion
with the essence of the earth.
The spirit of renewal
Engages transformation
A new genesis on the first day of Spring.
It is the season of our rebirth.
The peripatetic
seasons tell us there is no abiding place,
No durable peace.
All things fade away
Then Spring reminds us that
The Creator's motif is inflexible.
Life is renewed,
Revived in splendor.
Divine providence on display.
While earth whirls upon its accustomed path
Spring unveils immaculate poetic beauty.
The frost begins to thaw.
Gentle rains spread their mist.

We see the flower, once a secret in the seed.
Buds emerge, ready to bloom.
Birds return to build unsullied nests.
Leaves burst forth from waiting, hopeful trees.
Bulbs break through earth's custodial prison.
The chrysalis sets free the insect once
Crawling with many legs,
Now to fly flirtatiously with two colored wings.
Snowdrop flowers spread their fragrance in the fields,
After a winter of blizzard frenzy and drifting snowflakes.
The ice melts, running down hillside trails
swelling streams and tepid lakes.
The photosynthesis of life
In us are many changes.
We breathe in life.
We exhale life.
Springtime illumination.
We become exuberant, like creation
Integrated in our souls.
We manifest the purpose of Spring
We are not mere observes of beauty so sincere.
The splendor we see is amalgamated,
Into our soul, where joy rebounds.
Where love is found.
We are the new life we see.
We are part of the terrain
The world is part of us.
We become one in Spring.
We are a new creation.
Life breaks through our times of despair and darkness.

We have been becoming through our earthly years and seasons
God, with His creative Word,
His author's touch,
Makes us in His image.
"God is the poet, painter, singer, the sculptor and the architect," someone said.
Past years shape character.
The future fashions our dreams.
God, In the beginning, made the
Skies, stars, seas, sun, water, earth,
He shaped and assigned them to their proper place.
God breathed and birthed His designs into song.
His symphony pressed upon the reed to give the world its sound.
His Word to shape,
His finger to paint the landscape into color,
To sculpt chaos into form
To give us paradise and not parody.
The beauty we see, not a caricature of His thoughts
but the declaration of His nature.
We are created in His image!
With His mind in us, we reflect His world.
With no mind, but our own, we are merely imitations.
With His breath that gave us life,
We are promised, that through each moment
Here on earth,
In the varying season,
We will see the beauty of the world.
Know the magnificence of His love,
That has made us the crown of His creation,
A resurrection in us
Of His eternal Spring.

The Leaves Return In Springtime

The leaves that fell last autumn
in repose upon the ground
caught in blades of grass and weeds
as winds whipped them in a frenzy
and carried them away,
after months of shading the earth
in the heat of day
and cooling fevered bodies
on blankets in picnic banquets of
woodland and meadow fields of tranquility
releasing fresh air to breathe
now return through their familiar twigs and buds
with new life to redress
their dreary wintry barrenness
in anticipation of
verdant tenderness
their supple newness
ready for the blazing sun
or gentle evening breezes
providing protective nesting places
for birds that sing
and squirrels that dance
among the branches
and lovers who
chit chat, reclining against
the aging trunks

while reading books
beneath the outstretched
canopy of embracing limbs
in summertime shades
they are all new leaves
yet they bloom and grow
with new seasons and new promises,
that life returns
life goes on.
each season is short
but filled
with unexpected joys
in their three month
purpose of their living
But now is Springtime
and soon to be the dog days of summer
so catch the breeze
stand against the storm
offer shelter to those who seek
play games with the squirrels that chase
each other and hide
round the bark
in mating foreplay
stand beneath a tree
that pushes its new leaves
into a brand new day
look closely
tiny at first
watch them grow

form their shape and purpose
don't let a leaf go unnoticed
find a purpose in their budding
look at leaves,
tender new leaves
with a telescopic soul
and know
that
in each new
tender unfolding
there is something
in them, that reminds us of ourselves
within each of us
from deep within
emerges
new life.
in our seasons of living.
catch the breezes of life
feel the warmth of promise
release something of love from within your heart
to purify the air
with love
so all can breath in love
and exhale love
spread wide the limbs of your life
and send deep the roots of your joy
into creation's nourishing source
and in this season
become what you are meant to be

A Thousand Years From Now Will Someone Think of Me?

A Thousand Years From Now Will Someone Think of Me?
I can only imagine an ancestor's face.
There are no pictures to see any resemblance
Of the face that now stares at me in the mirror.
Did they look like me?
If I contemplate enough,
Discerning a deep lasting truth,
I see their lives around me.
I need only touch my skin.
In the epidermis layers are all the unknown seasons, all the unknown people.
All their DNA that comprises me.
Their spirit is the thread of love through the passing time.
I see their lifeforce in many ways.
Stones make the babbling brook sing. I hear them.
Wind gives leaves their voice in the breeze of Spring. I feel them.
Wounds of life make the soul lament and cry. I empathize with them.
A fear, touched by hope, can find rest. Perhaps my love can give them peace.
Thoughts held dear can fill the world with joy. I laugh with them.
A mind that dreams dares to look at bright horizons. I share their vision.
We live. We learn. The years we have are few,
Save for a few people we know,
The earth will never know our name.
Will it matter that we have lived?
Or that we have touched someone
With words of love
On our shared path along the way?

Will I be remembered?
How can I promise not to forget
To walk beside the one who wonders
If their life has any purpose
As they seem to travel, like us, alone?
Just to hear someone call our name!
Just to be remembered.
Or to others a kindness show?
Someday all the photos in a box of memories
Will be thrown away, along with once held treasures.
Some having an extended life because of the digital world.
We will come to know that in this brief time,
To have lived at all, is what matters, even if we are forgotten.
To have shared the sacred air we breathe
Close enough to another, a stranger unknown
A lover loved.
To hear the essence of who we are and awaken to this truth…
There is a song in
The breeze
The lament
The cry
The dream
The peace
The name spoken
The heartbeat felt,
of each other.
With our promise not to forget
While so many pass away like a dream.
Though the pictures of all our seasons
Are tossed away,
The heart keeps beating.
Beating, Beating

Singing
Hopeful, that in the moments beyond
when we are no more
That the breeze among the leaves
the song among the brook
Within the dreams left behind that somehow survive
through each lament and cry of time
in all these things we will be,
that we will have been,
even if
we are not remembered,
our faces never known.
Or through a touch of a button consigned, forgotten to a cloud.
I hear the brook
I feel the breeze
I promise you
That I will think,
For just a moment,
And see through my eyes
And know that through the song in my ears
And what I see with my own eyes
That you are here,
That you have been,
In this moment
With me.
I pray someday
A thousand years hence
Someone will think of me this way.
A thousand ages are like an evening gone.
As I stare silently in the space before me, or reflected in the brook
In the consciousness beyond myself, I will think of you, though I know not your name.
Will someone think of me this way when a thousand seasons pass?

The Doe

Like a gentle deer
In the secret wood
Finds its place of trust
In soft beds of waving grass;
Where life unfolds with
Wonders before its startled eyes,
With dreams so real displayed,
A solitude and paradise of peace
To fall in love with falling rivers
Besides the running streams
That flow to quench its thirst,
My spirit, like the innocent Doe
Seeks a gentle, reassuring place
Where no fear resides
In the beauty of surprising gifts like
Butterflies that dance on fields of flowers
As sunlight warms their place of
Rest beneath the arms of
Shielding trees.
Oh how I need this peace to seep into my yearning needs.
Alert, upon the woodland path
It seeks to teach me to long

For quiet moments
to still my mind.
To help me look within my heart
And know that
Like the gentle, trusting Doe,
Besides the still waters of my dreams
that love is
Always near,
Wherever I may roam,
Among Eden paths.
Standing still, the Doe turns to look into my eyes
Daring me to follow on the path
That leads to secret places in the woods,
And hidden places in my soul,
Where joy dwells
in living streams
Of love.
Now I can find a rest
In the waving grass.
And thank the Deer
Who did, one day,
My life pass.

(Listen to Michel Pepe's Music about the Deer La Biche d'Amour - YouTube)

Changing Moon, Changing Tides, Changing Lives and Changing Seasons

A dark sea can evoke deep fear
when standing before its mysterious depths.
Tides and currents threaten us like pursuing footsteps
on a shadowy path or alleyway.
But then a star and moon breaks through the clouds
to lay an encouraging illumination upon the ebony surface
as if to chase away some lurking creature
with reassurance that its robe of light
upon the surface, summons us to step upon a path of hope
to carry us in its shimmering promise
that lifts the heart on cresting waves
that rush their luminosity toward us.
Beneath our feet
the churning brilliance of light surround us with
arcane thoughts of love and life
that swirl around our feet and splashes 'round our knees
and flows within our hearts
until we are emersed in living water
as the tide secures our feet
firmly in the sand.
The gift of the moon glistens like gems and words of wisdom,
like diamond facets sparkling upon the sea of our imagination.

In prose, in poems and feelings the moon speaks to our spirit
in the concert of its symphony upon the shore
so we can learn of life, to know ourselves, to discover one another
and to claim in these celestial reflections a sea of love
a sea of solitude
of yearnings deep
with the ocean's bright illuminations and rising tides and lower ebbs
seeking to pull us into the currents of its light cast upon the dark.
The moonlight guides our drifting lives
till we find out who we are
in this rhythmic flow of life.
We hear within a crashing wave a message of the reason for our living and our loving
The moon speaks to us as it throws its words and brightness upon the water.
We dance upon the ocean's swelling waves
and let the light swell in our hearts, revealing hidden secrets, and yearning dreams
illuminating deep within our souls
something of the Creator's wonder
that made us who we are.
We wonder, as we look upon the Sun, the moon, the stars,
the starfish, the sea, the waves, the sand, the shells,
Who are we, that He made us, that He saved us
With a love more vast
than the widest sea.
We hold a shell to our ear and hear His voice
We hold the light to our heart
and are carried upon His crest of love and
through all the tempests of the sea and changing tides
and all the changing seasons of our lives,
within God's light and depth of love
we always will abide.

Look at the World

by John Rutter

Look at the world: Everything all around us
Look at the world: and marvel everyday
Look at the world: So many joys and wonders
So many miracles along our way
Praise to thee o lord for all creation
Give us thankful hearts that we may see
All the gifts we share and every blessing
All things come of thee
Look at the earth: Bringing forth fruit and flower
Look at the sky: The sunshine and the rain
Look at the hills, look at the trees and mountains
Valley and flowing river field and plain
Praise to thee o lord for all creation
Give us thankful hearts that we may see
All the gifts we share and every blessing
All things come of thee
Think of the spring,

Think of the warmth of summer
Bringing the harvest before the winters cold
Everything grows, everything has a season
Til' it is gathered to the fathers fold
Praise to thee o lord for all creation
Give us thankful hearts that we may see
All the gifts we share and every blessing
All things come of thee
Every good gift, all that we need and cherish
Comes from the lord in token of his love
We are his hands, stewards of all his bounty
His is the earth and his the heavens above
Praise to thee, o lord for all creation
Give us thankful hearts that we may see
All the gifts we share, and every blessing
All things come of thee
All things come of thee

Songwriters:
Pardon Simbarashe Charandurah.

John Rutter, Composer

(Available on YouTube Music)

Summer and winter and springtime and harvest

Sun, moon and stars in their courses above

Join with all nature in manifold witness

To Thy great faithfulness, mercy and love

Great is Thy faithfulness

Great is Thy faithfulness

Morning by morning new mercies I see

All I have needed Thy hand hath provided

Great is Thy faithfulness, Lord, unto me

(from the hymn, Great Is Thy Faithfulness, lyrics by Thomas O. Chisholm)

God of Our Life
Through All The Circling Years

God of our life, through all the circling years,
we trust in you;
in all the past, through all our hopes and fears,
your hand we view.
With each new day, when morning lifts the veil,
we own your mercies, Lord, which never fail.

God of the past, our times are in your hand;
with us abide.
Lead us by faith, to hope's true Promised Land;
be now our guide.
With you to bless, the darkness shines as light,
and faith's fair vision changes into sight.

God of the coming years, thro' paths unknown
we follow you;
when we are strong, Lord, leave us not alone;
our faith renew.
Be now for us in life our daily bread,
our heart's true home when all our years have sped.

(Hugh Thomson Kerr and Charles H. Purdy, lyrics, composer)

God Is Unchanging

Seasons change
But God's love
Never changes.
It becomes more wondrous in the variable seasons of our lives.
Intensifies!
Grows!
Unfolds!
Matures!
The temporal becomes immortal.
Time manifests itself into being.
We live in God.
God lives in us.

A breath ceases
A heart becomes still
Warmth begins to chill
Touch losses its feeling
Eyes stare without seeing
Sound becomes silent
Hearing fades into a distant void
Absorbed into unborn moments
Movement petrifies
Music turns to rest,
Anticipating new measures, new melodies, new symphonies

A changeless Spirit plans rebirth
A hand touches its fingerprint upon new creations
Touches us
We are called to new life.
The song and seasons go on
We are born for a new season.
We discover ourselves
changing, becoming, forming
All things become new
As all things change.
We are mystified.
God is unchanging
God is creator
God is eternal changelessness
Essence
Spirit
Love
Love never ends
It is forever beginning
Creating a world of new seasons
New mercies
Every morning

Wondrous moments
Life into being
While all things fade away
With each passing season
Eternity is in each moment,
In each instant
In us
Love breathed into us
The unalterable love of God
So that we might receive the promised joys
Of the wondrous seasons of our lives,
The wondrous grace of God.
The promise that while seasons change
And we move through each wondrous moment
The hand that created us
Promises the greatest, wondrous gift –
A fuller season -
Eternal life.
That will never change!
It is what God intends
For all creation.
What wondrous love – this is!

$\mathcal{E}$pilogue

Listen Carefully to the Silence of The Seasons

"IF YOU LISTEN CAREFULLY THE SILENCE IS BEAUTIFUL"

The thought made me reflect on a few thoughts about being in a silent mood. Being carefully intentional in what the silence was revealing to my senses. After about an hour I wrote a few reflections regarding what I was hearing in the silence. From my thoughts to pen flowed these images:

Carefully. Intentionally. Purposely. Careful listening requires contemplation. To listen doesn't necessarily mean to be inactive….listening to silence…. The Silence is Beautiful.

Listening to a leaf waving in a gentle breeze. Listening is the observation of a drifting cloud in the sky overhead, a reminder that motion is silent. The drifting tufts of white, caught within the jet streams of currents and weather patterns. The silence of a sun ray breaking through forest trees that comes to rest on green fern and moss….. stepping upon the velvet carpet with warmth that touches nature and our face…..a twinkling star at night suspended in the dark universe, speaks of silent beauty in celestial corridors. Eyes that stare into the imperceptible depth of our hidden soul….that stare and listen to the still voice of love within. A spider spinning webs of silent lace that holds the beauty of morning dew. Tiny blue eggs within a nest, in silence, waiting for an impending birth. A touch that holds no words but gives unexpressed comfort when pain is deep and grief unbearable. Hands that hold and speak encouragement when loneliness speaks louder than our solitude. Quiet lakes that hold reflections of shoreline trees, tall mountains, clouds and skies, that double the silent beauty. Cathedral naves without the sound of organ swells or clergy oratory or whispered prayers, but only sunlight through colored glass infusing silence with sacred strokes of a Creator's touch that cast their colored prisms on marble floors and stone columns..

Listen carefully. All this silence is beautiful. Such things, carefully heard in the silence, in the silence of our minds, sustain us in the silent seasons of our lives.

My prayer for you, as we move through the beauty of each Season of Summer, Winter, Fall and Spring, is that you might find many moments to be silent. To be careful to listen. The Silence is Beautiful. Hear the still small voice of God in the silence of your thoughts and contemplations.....and thank God for the wondrous seasons of our lives.

A Closing Love Letter
In This Season Of Joy!

To all my readers:

Like snowflakes, the memories drift around my mind, softly falling upon my heart. My tears that fall upon the accumulation of my emotions crystalize like diamonds that capture the sparkling images of loving faces, that speak with silent voices through their eyes as I remember treasured moments through my life.

They come to me, through silent pictures. Their presence is felt in familiar surroundings, when the touch of candle glow flickers in remembrance before their picture and candlelight on windowsills illuminate the warmth that holds me. The twinkling lights on trees and shrubs outside the window still help me feel, that as the passing years move along without their loving touch, that I am not alone. Their love, like those lights, keep me warm against the absence of their lives. In the harsh silence of my sadness and the silent snow, I hear their whispers. Like the sudden wind that turns the drifting snow in new pathways as they fall, I realize, that through my life, in my life, they are still near. Still here. But move around like unsuspecting grace to make their presence felt among my longing thoughts that come to me in surprising ways, falling gently upon my spirit.

There, before my heart, lies their presence to comfort my uncertainties with their reassuring essence. Love knows no bounds, nor has constrictions forced upon my life, as in my solitude I think of them. Their spirit helps me to feel the stillness. To slip into the silence, where we hold each other. When love is felt how can one feel an emptiness within? Love is only intensified. How, in someone's absence, that person sustains our silence, with a tranquil comfort, so that even when tears flood our eyes, and run down our cheeks to rest upon a quivering lip, we realize resting upon our lips is a kiss to reassure us that their love has no end.

How love can melt and be drawn into a soundless tear. A thought comes to mind. A tear comes to the eye. A word speaks to the heart. We marvel how wisdom still instructs us through echoes of conversation. How healing embraces us when we think of a parent's arms that held us, their hands that helped us find happiness in their grasp. Pictures now hold our thankful hearts and every blessing.

In my silence alone, the silence of the season, when snow dances in the swirling wind, I grab hold of a memory, let the flickering candle glow shine within my eyes and feel your love still dancing around with joy to remind me of this: that even when alone, within the glowing light, and the season's joy, there is a deep inner peace. I feel this when I think of those no longer here. To see a tree with lights. Trains beneath the tree. On a Christmas morn. And a manger in the center of it all.

At Christmas time, this feeling has a tenacious hold. There comes to mind the peace and light, the memory, the reality, that Light came down to earth, so that we might see among the falling snow of this silent night the peace and calm that holds us in the Light that falls upon the snow, that illuminates our souls. The peace that comes when we fall upon God's heart. In a manger stall. On this Christmas Day. As we hold all these memories dear, that we have loved through all our years. Just hold this thought close to your heart, that when the Christ Child was born, should we not think, that in His birth, we found the gift, that God was kissing us with love? May you find love, be love, in all the wondrous seasons of your life.

Ronald W. Cadmus

"Be present O merciful God, and protect us through

The silent hours of this night, so that we who are

Wearied by the work and the changes of this fleeting world
may rest upon Thy eternal changelessness."

(An Ancient Collect)

"In every change, God faithful will remain."

("Be Still My Soul" Hymn)

"Change and decay all around me I see, but Thou who

Changest not, abide with me"

("Abide With Me" Hymn)

There Is Beauty Everywhere

By Ronald W. Cadmus

A butterfly's fluttering wing
A soaring bird with wings that catch the breeze
A leaf carried by a brook or stream
A candle brightly burning without a flicker
A touch that soothes a pain
A kiss resting gently on one's cheek
A drop of rain sliding on a window pane
A morning mist covering a spider web
A canoe gliding on a tranquil lake
A bird snugged comfortably on a brooding nest
A sound of loons in a woodland fog
A twinkling star
A quiet hush of waves on the shore
A melody hummed in the heart
A loved one held in a memory
A ray of sun through forest trees
The presence of God's Spirit that stills my soul,
That gives me peace,
That fills me with love.
Everywhere!
Everywhere!
There is beauty everywhere.

About The Author

Ronald W. Cadmus was ordained a United Methodist Minister in 1975. He is a graduate of West Virginia Wesleyan College and Drew Theological Seminary. He was installed as the 48th Minister in Line of Succession at the Historic Collegiate Church of New York City, America's oldest congregation founded in 1628, under the invitation of Dr. Norman Vincent Peale, the author of *The Power of Positive Thinking* and Senior Minister of the Collegiate Church. He served as Minister of The Fort Washington Collegiate Church of the Reformed Church in America. The Church was recognized as Church of The Year by Prison Fellowship for its outreach ministry to inmates and their families. Ron is the author *of God's Loving Embrace: The Touch That Comforts and Restores, (published by Thomas Nelson) Still, In One Peace* and *Fragile Ornaments, Melting Snowflakes and The Healing Light of Christmas (Published by Circle Books).* Thomas Nelson Publishers includes several of Ron's inspiring writings in the book *A Deeper Walk,* featuring writings of outstanding Christian Leaders in America. Ron Cadmus has produced choral anthems with Joseph Martin, Kevin Boesiger, Douglas Wagner, Robert S. Cohen, Brad Nix, Margaret Rizza of London, Mario Lombardo (with Warner Brothers), Michael Huseman, Michael Bussewitz-Quarm, Dan Wolgemuth and Steve Mugglin. A number of his works in collaboration with Robert S. Cohen have been written for and premiered by The Philadelphia Boys Choir – Young Ambassadors of the United States, who also premiered their major 42 minute work, GENESIS, We Lift Our Voice and Celebrate. Robert Cohen's masterful work, *Safe Places of The Heart,* a text written by Ron Cadmus in Memory of those killed at The Pulse Nightclub in Orlando, Florida, won the first prize competition at the Harrisburg GMC celebrating their 30th Anniversary and was also performed at the Commemorative Celebrations of the Arizona Memorial in Pearl Harbor as a statement of the cause of freedom for which so many people have sacrificed their lives and given their service. Ron served as a Chaplain at Ground Zero following 9/11 and his prose about his experience appears on the Artist's Registry of the World Trade Center Museum. Also published by Hal Leonard, Shawnee Publishers and Santa Barbara Press are the choral works, *The Gift of Dreams to Dream, The Beauty of Life, The Joy of Simple Things and The Gift of Advent Waiting* for which Ron wrote the lyrics. His work, *The Silence of Forgiveness* (The Prodigal Son) composed by Jen Wagner was recently premiered by Lebanon Valley University Choir. Ms. Wagner is also producing a major choral work, *The Softened Strings of Violins* in recognition of the present war in Ukraine. Mr. Michael Huseman, is setting Ron's text, *I Want To Go Home*, remembering the children of Ukraine. Ron's book *The Melodies of Christ,* was published by Thomas Nelson, Zondervan/Westbow Press. It is a compilation of lyrics, prose and liturgy that deals with the blending of Contemporary and Traditional aspects of Worship in creative ways. Presently, Ron is providing pulpit supply for the Reformed Church in America.

About The Illustrator

Carol Bicknell says about her work, "I have been drawn to and inspired by the Impressionists. My preferred media had always been watercolors but now I enjoy exploring many different media such as, charcoal, watercolor, acrylics, acrylic ink, pen and ink, oil pastel and soft pastel. I like to work with these mediums separately and combined. I experiment with different papers, such as rough, hot press, or cold press watercolor papers, Yupo, and mineral paper, to give different effects to my work. I also enjoy the process of making collage with painted papers that I have created. Also, making monotypes that involve painting on a printing plate to make a one-of-a-kind print. I work intuitively resulting in what I call abstract impressions informed by a lifetime of visual experiences. I am drawn to the beauty of nature: the sky, the weather, clouds, trees and flowers. I endeavor to paint from my heart and allow it to flow onto the paper."

Ron Cadmus and Carol Bicknell are neighbors in the historic town of Ocean Grove, NJ at the Jersey Shore.

Printed in the United States
by Baker & Taylor Publisher Services